T0016741

THE

GHOSTLY TALES

OF

ALCATRAZ

Published by Arcadia Children's Books
A Division of Arcadia Publishing
Charleston, SC
www.arcadiapublishing.com

Copyright © 2023 by Arcadia Children's Books
All rights reserved

Spooky America is a trademark of Arcadia Publishing, Inc.

First published 2023

Manufactured in the United States

All images used courtesy of Shutterstock.com; p. 38 Naeblys/Shutterstock.com;
p. 72 Joel McCartan/Shutterstock.com.

ISBN 978-1-4671-9732-8

Library of Congress Control Number: 2023931840

Notice: The information in this book is true and complete to the best of our
knowledge. It is offered without guarantee on the part of the author or Arcadia
Publishing. The author and Arcadia Publishing disclaim all liability in connection with
the use of this book.

All rights reserved. No part of this book may be reproduced or transmitted in any form
whatsoever without prior written permission from the publisher except in the case of
brief quotations embodied in critical articles and reviews.

Spooky America

THE GHOSTLY TALES OF ALCATRAZ

STACIA DEUTSCH

Adapted from *Ghosts and Legends of Alcatraz*
by Bob Davis and Brian Clune

arcadia
CHILDREN'S BOOKS

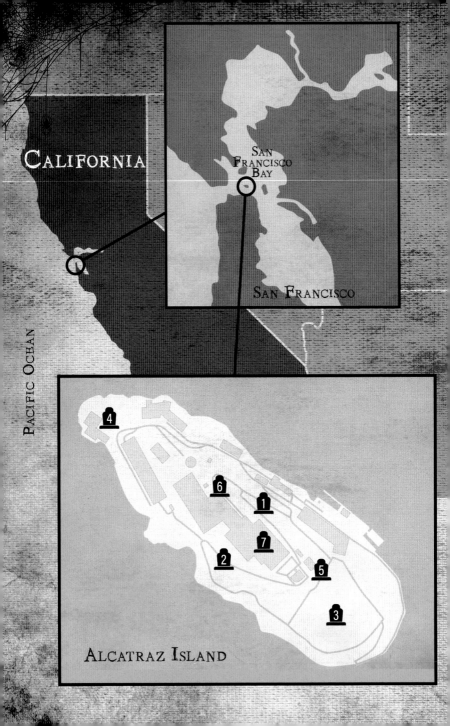

CALIFORNIA

SAN FRANCISCO BAY

SAN FRANCISCO

PACIFIC OCEAN

ALCATRAZ ISLAND

TABLE OF CONTENTS & MAP KEY

Welcome to Spooky Alcatraz!

In the heart of the San Francisco Bay, more than a mile offshore, sits a small, rocky, world-famous island. With its rich history, rugged cliffs, and breathtaking views of the San Francisco skyline, it's no wonder people come from all over the world to visit.

But be warned, Reader: this is no island paradise.

On the contrary, *this* island was once home to some of the world's most dangerous criminals. A federal prison surrounded by frigid, shark-infested waters, so perilous that no one has ever escaped and lived to tell the tale. (That we know of.) In fact, this island is so spooky, and *so* full of ghosts, it's considered one of the most haunted places in America.

Welcome to Alcatraz.

With all the ghostly things that have happened here, it's no wonder that Alcatraz, otherwise known as "The Rock," is so popular with ghost hunters and paranormal researchers. Not to mention tourists, since every year more than a million people board ferries and flock to the island. They come to see the historic buildings of the old federal prison that opened in 1934. They come to see art exhibits and installations. They come for the incredible views of San Francisco, one of

California's busiest cities. But maybe most of all, they come for the ghosts.

Lots and *lots* of ghosts.

Where did all these spooks come from? And how did a barren rock in the middle of the San Francisco Bay become so world-famous? The answer will take us on a tour through history, all the way from melting glaciers and Indigenous legends, to famous gangsters and crazy escape attempts.

Some people say the spooky stories about Alcatraz are just tall tales or legends to make the island feel more mysterious than it really is. But what if the legends are true? During the nearly thirty years the prison was in operation (1934–1963), more than 1,500 criminals spent time on Alcatraz. What if the reports of moaning voices, echoing clangs, and heavy footsteps really *are* the ghosts of former prisoners? What if the strange scents filling the hallways aren't due to the damp ocean air and decaying cellblocks but, rather, a spooky presence still lingering on the island after all these years?

And it's not just the ghosts of prisoners that linger at The Rock. There have been sightings of evil beasts and deadly spirits haunting the island long before it was turned into a prison, and even long before the Spanish arrived to colonize the area.

We may never know for sure, but what we do know is that Alcatraz holds many, *many*

secrets—starting with the Indigenous peoples who have lived in the area for thousands of years, all the way up to the time when Alcatraz held some of the most hardened prisoners under lock and key. Which is precisely why ghost hunters and paranormal researchers love to investigate the island. You might think that when Alcatraz became a huge tourist destination, the ghosts would have slipped quietly away to avoid the crowds, but instead, more and more people reported sightings of strange and spooky things.

In the spring of 1973, Planet Paranormal founder, Bob Davis, went to Alcatraz with his family for a day of sightseeing. Bob was only

thirteen years old at the time. While on the tour of the jail cells, his family came to Cellblock D, which had five spaces for solitary confinement (a form of imprisonment in which a prisoner lives in a single cell by themselves for days or even weeks). When the guide asked who wanted to step into a cell, Bob excitedly volunteered.

Once inside, the guide closed the door to show what the darkness would feel like to a prisoner. Immediately, Bob felt a grip on his shoulder and heard a voice whisper in his ear: *"You're mine!"* He pounded on the door and begged the guard to let him out.

That day, Bob's life changed forever. He learned more about the paranormal world, wanting to discover all he could about Alcatraz Island's history. Today, through his work, Bob Davis has spoken to many people who have seen ghosts at Alcatraz. They share that the island feels like it's soaked in despair, longing, and fear. Certainly, some spirits from the past have memories of happier times, but those memories are pushed back into the shadows by those for whom Alcatraz was a place of sorrow and pain.

There's no telling when the ghosts of Alcatraz Island will appear. Sometimes, it's at night. Spirits glow through the dark and eerie fog. Sightings are common when the winds howl and fierce waves hit the steep cliffs. But the bright sunshine can also lure the mysteries of the island out of the shadows.

If you want to know more about the history of Alcatraz and the tormented souls that refuse to leave the island, read on ...

The Ohlone and Evil Spirits

Imagine a time when the San Francisco Bay was not filled with water. It was dry land. During that geologic period, the islands that now dot the bay were mountain peaks. Indigenous people, called the Ohlone, roamed the area searching for food and firewood. As time passed, glaciers melted and the sea level began to rise. Water filled the area and tribes moved to the mainland, but the Ohlone maintained their connection to two special mountains that had become islands.

It's impossible to know exactly how the tribes used the islands, but legend says the Ohlone made the island into a fishing base. Legend *also* says they were the first to use the land as an early prison. The Ohlone sent people who committed crimes there to keep them away from the rest of the tribe. Since the only way on or off the island was by boat, they could isolate anyone who broke tribal law. As more prisoners were sent to the island, the fishermen began to avoid it. They claimed there was evil lurking there and the criminals were attracting the ghosts of unhappy ancestors.

And then, the island became even creepier.

The most respected position in the tribe was the shaman. The shaman was thought to have supernatural powers. It was the shaman's responsibility to heal the sick, lead the tribe in rites and rituals, and keep everyone safe from evil spirits and enemies. As rumors of ghosts swirled, a shaman decided he needed to look for sorcerers and witches hiding among the tribe on the mainland. If he believed someone had unusual powers, he had two choices: either send them to live in isolation on the island . . . or kill them. Some people were forced to stay in isolation until they died naturally. Sometimes, the shaman also sent dead bodies to the island. In time, the spirit population there grew.

Rumors spread that the island's spirits wanted revenge on the shamans who had sent them there to die. If they couldn't get to the shamans, they'd go after the fishermen, or anyone who came too close. The spirits didn't only want to scare the living—they wanted them to suffer, just as they had.

In 1775, the first Spanish ship entered the

bay and the Spaniards gave names to the two islands they saw. They called the larger one *La Isla de los Ángeles* (Angel Island). The smaller island was home to a large number of seabirds, so they named it *La Isla de los Alcatraces* (Alcatraz is the Spanish word for pelican). The name was eventually shortened to Alcatraz.

The Spanish set up a missionary system along the coast to spread the teachings of the Roman Catholic Church. This system was the end of the Ohlone's way of life. The Ohlone were forced to convert to Catholicism or face death. The Spanish also brought new diseases with them. By 1830, there were fewer than two thousand Ohlone left.

Some Ohlone tried to escape the Spaniards. They went to the one place they knew the Spanish wouldn't go.

The Spanish were afraid of Alcatraz Island because they also believed ghosts lived there. That's what made Alcatraz the perfect place to hide out: the Spanish would never set foot on the island. The Ohlone who dared to go to Alcatraz Island built small villages, and their tiny community survived for many years.

By 1834, the Spanish mission system ended, but there were hardly any Ohlone left. As more and more settlers came to America and moved westward with the Gold Rush, the situation for any remaining Ohlone and other indigenous populations worsened. Lands were stolen, forced slavery continued, and many people were killed. Alcatraz was no longer a safe place to hide.

When the United States bought California as part of the 1848 Treaty of Guadalupe Hidalgo, they made plans to convert Alcatraz Island into a military fort to protect the bay from invaders.

This meant the end of the Indigenous peoples' ownership of the island. The military fort was converted to a maximum-security prison in the 1930s. And when the federal government shut down the prison in 1963 and abandoned the island, a group made up of Indigenous peoples saw it as an opportunity to take control of Alcatraz once again.

In 1969, seventy-nine Native Americans landed on Alcatraz and claimed the island. A standoff between the occupiers and the U.S. government finally ended eighteen months later, on June 10, 1971, when U.S. Marshals, the FBI, and local police arrested the people on Alcatraz.

The protest didn't work the way the occupiers had hoped, but it did bring attention to the long history of Indigenous peoples on the island. Around the country, the government began to take a fresh look at the rights of indigenous tribes. Some say the occupation on Alcatraz was the spark for the modern Native American Civil Rights Movement.

Today, signs of the island's indigenous history can still be found around Alcatraz, but only the wandering spirits know the whole truth of what happened there.

That is, the spirits . . . and the *others*.

According to legend, there are other creatures on Alcatraz who protected the Ohlone from harm. Creatures who also know the history of the island, because they've been there all along.

One creature, as the Spanish learned, was even out for blood.

Colonization and the Island Beasts

As the Spanish continued to mistreat the Ohlone, more and more of them decided to escape and hide on the islands in the bay, including Alcatraz. Even though the Ohlone believed evil spirits inhabited the island, many felt they'd rather take their chances with the spirits than suffer abuse from the Spanish. And the Ohlone knew the Spaniards had their own fears about evil things that might be lurking on the island, including a red-eyed monster known as Matah Kagmi.

Matah Kagmi is a term Indigenous peoples use for Sasquatch, also known as Bigfoot. Legends of Bigfoot go back so far in time, no one knows where they actually began. Native Americans shared stories that said the creatures were smart and sympathetic. Some of the Ohlone people who fled to the island hoped the Matah Kagmi would protect them from evil.

One popular story told of an indigenous man who was walking down a deer trail when a creature approached. The creature was completely covered in thick, rough hair and smelled like dirt and moss. The man knew immediately he had come face-to-face with a Matah Kagmi.

The creature bellowed and the man froze in place. The two stared at each other. There was a softness in the creature's eyes that told the man he was not in danger. The man gave the Matah Kagmi the fish he was carrying. The hairy creature took the offering and hurried back to the woods. But before he disappeared completely, he turned and made a long, low sound. Perhaps it was a way of saying *Thank you*?

A few weeks later, the same man heard a sound outside his cabin. When he went to investigate, he found a stack of deer skins, ready for tanning. He didn't see who had left them, but he heard the same long, low sound echoing through the trees.

Years later, the man found himself in terrible danger. He had been bitten by a rattlesnake, and because there was no way to get rid of the poison in his blood, he figured he would die.

The man passed out, but when he woke up, he found three Matah Kagmi standing over him. It felt like a dream, though the man knew it was real. They had found a way to draw out the venom and had even packed his wound with healing herbs and plants.

The man never saw the creatures again, but he often heard their call.

From this story and others like it, the idea spread among the Ohlone and other Indigenous peoples that the Matah Kagmi protected their friends. The idea also spread that the Matah Kagmi could be vicious to those they felt were enemies.

The Spanish believed in the Matah Kagmi and were afraid. But they were *also* afraid of the Bukwus—an even more frightening and dangerous creature they believed roamed Alcatraz. Some people confuse the Matah

Kagmi and the Bukwus, but they aren't the same.

It's said the Bukwus are the corpses of people who drowned near the rocks and stayed on the island. These evil creatures are like zombies. They are hairy with peeling skin, matted hair, and an appetite for small children.

The Bukwus live in the forest, by streams, lakes, and rivers. They have great physical strength and the ability to become invisible so they can sneak up on people. If a Bukwus finds a living person, they can drown them and turn them into a Bukwus, too. Or they can feed them a special ghostly food that converts the living to the dead.

In some of the legends, the Bukwus' eyes turn red when they want to eat. This has led to many stories of a red-eyed monster on the island. The Ohlone and the Spanish saw the glowing red eyes, and the legend continues to this day. There are many who say they have seen red-eyed creatures on Alcatraz. In fact, there are rumored to be many Bukwus hiding around the shoreline.

In 1822, Mexico took control of this area of North America from the Spanish. The Mexicans were not interested in the Indigenous peoples,

nor the islands in the San Francisco Bay. They never talked about the Matah Kagmi or the Bukwus and so, the stories and legends about evil spirits and beastly creatures living on Alcatraz died down.

But when this territory became part of the United States in 1850, that all changed . . .

Mysterious Guns and Drums

In 1848, a man named James W. Marshall saw something glimmering in a creek at Sutter's Mill in Coloma, California, about 130 miles northeast of San Francisco. To his surprise, he had discovered gold! The news of his discovery spread, and before long, nearly 300,000 people flocked to California and the San Francisco Bay Area in what became known as the California Gold Rush.

As more and more people settled there, San Francisco became an important center of trade, and the U.S. government worried that foreign invaders would try to take the land. The government built a fort on Alcatraz Island that was meant to hold back invading ships coming from the bay.

In 1861, the American Civil War began. This war wasn't fought anywhere near California, but politicians worried the Pacific Coast could be a target for both the Confederacy and the British because of the area's rich gold mines. The Union Army brought cannons to Alcatraz, and the island's fort, or citadel, grew. The prison also grew, as deserters, protestors, and Confederate prisoners were often sent to the island.

At the time, the prison was nothing more than a cement holding tank under a guardhouse. It was cold and drafty. Many prisoners got sick.

When a tuberculosis outbreak struck the prison, nurses from San Francisco were called to the island to help. One of the nurses who came to aid the prisoners contracted the disease. Authorities wouldn't let her leave the island and she sadly died there, along with many of the prisoners she had tried to heal. It's said that among the spirits of Alcatraz, this nurse still haunts the halls, eternally searching for a way to serve others.

After the Civil War, the U.S. government decided to build up the fortifications (defensive walls) on the island. They created new platforms and higher walls, brought in more guns, and built a bombproof barracks for soldiers. On the southeast side of the island, permanent living quarters and parade grounds were constructed. There are rumors that the government built secret tunnels to crisscross the entire island, and even though this has been proven false, many still believe the tunnels exist.

In time, the government began cutting back on the amount of money it allocated to Alcatraz, and by 1877, funding was stopped altogether. By 1901, the purpose of the island had changed. It was no longer a military fort. Alcatraz was now a home for military prisoners. And the number of prisoners sent to the island kept on growing.

The military personnel on the island had to look after the prisoners, so they were no longer required to be on watch for outside attacks. There was less happening on the island, and it got a bit quiet. But while the military activity decreased, the spooky activity *increased*. Soldiers reported hearing ghostly sounds and seeing strange creatures. It was as if during the busy times on the island, the supernatural beings retreated; but now, in the relative quiet, they were free to come out again.

One of the first reports of something odd on the island came in 1902. A trooper reported hearing the sound of drums coming from the parade grounds. He said that the banging was loud and steady, so he went to investigate. As he approached the grounds, the sounds got louder and louder. But the instant his foot touched the parade area, the noise stopped. No one was there. He never heard the drums again.

Another story came from a captain who was making rounds on the island at night. He heard a steady drumbeat by the dock. At first, the captain thought that some of his men were playing a prank on him. When he reached the dock, he expected to see his men laughing, but instead he found one soldier guarding the area, as if everything were normal. He asked the man about the drums, but the man hadn't heard anything unusual.

The strangest story about the phantom drumbeats comes later, when the island was a federal prison. During World War II, Alcatraz was used as a torpedo and mine storage location. One night, after a ship dropped off new supplies, five soldiers heard the sound of drums. They went to see what was going on. The noise had come from the back of the wharf. When the soldiers arrived, they discovered a group of Indigenous peoples. Some were sitting around a fire; others were dancing around it.

The soldiers approached the group to tell them it was against the law to be on the island and that they needed to leave. But as the soldiers got closer, the entire scene vanished into thin air.

Over the years, prisoners, guards, and park rangers have reported hearing drums and seeing dancers. Prisoners also claimed to see Indigenous peoples walking the halls of the prison. Perhaps these were the spirits of those sent to the island for punishment? Or maybe they were the determined spirits of those who came to escape the Spanish?

Other stories involve the sound of gunshots and cannon fire. After the Civil War, soldiers stationed on Alcatraz heard loud noises and thought they were under attack. They hurried to check it out but found no ships in the bay, nor any troops invading the island. There was apparently nothing to worry about.

Park rangers, tour guides, and visitors have heard even

more intense battles on the island. Some say that along with the gunfire, they hear soldiers running, cannons firing, and painful screams. They say it all ends within minutes and then . . . there's nothing. Just an eerie quiet and the softest whisper of the wind.

The battle ghosts are the strangest things to explain because Alcatraz was actually never the site of fighting. These sounds remain a mystery, but there are so many people who have witnessed them that they cannot simply be dismissed. Something strange, involving the memories of dead soldiers, is being replayed late at night on the island.

The question is . . . by *whom*?

Do you remember the stories of the Matah Kagmi and Bukwus that were rumored to live on the island? Well, there are many people who have reported seeing a red-eyed monster roaming the shoreline. Some insist it's one of these two creatures. Or perhaps there is another, even spookier supernatural being that lives on the island? No one knows for sure, but for more than a century, stories have been told (and continue to be told) about red-eyed creatures on Alcatraz.

After the 1906 fire that devastated San Francisco, it became clear that Alcatraz needed fire-resistant housing for the growing prisoner population. The army began to build new concrete barracks above the old bomb-proof ones. A huge cellhouse was built over the old citadel. It had four separate cellblocks. Alcatraz now had six hundred cells. By the time it was finished in 1912, the prison was the largest reinforced concrete building in the world.

Around the time of the Great Depression—a period of great economic hardship when many banks failed and money was tight—the Federal Government decided to pull the army out of Alcatraz for good. Alcatraz was expensive to maintain because it was an island, and all food, water, and supplies needed to be brought in by

boat. Most of the prisoners were sent away to another prison at Fort Leavenworth in Kansas, but Alcatraz officials decided to leave behind enough guards and staff to watch over the island's thirty-two most hardened criminals.

From that point on, until the day the prison closed in 1963, Alcatraz became a place of desperate men, legendary killers, and ghostly tales to rival your spookiest nightmares.

Cellblock at Alcatraz

CHAPTER 4

Escape from Alcatraz

It's said that no one has ever escaped from the federal prison at Alcatraz.

The truth is, nobody really knows.

(Can *you* imagine having to swim more than a mile in freezing cold water infested with great white sharks to escape from prison?)

Still, as rare as escape attempts were, during Alcatraz's twenty-nine years as a federal prison, there were fourteen escape attempts made by thirty-six prisoners. Two men tried twice. Twenty-three inmates were caught before getting far. At least three drowned. Seven were shot and killed. Five escaped prisoners were never found. They are presumed dead, but no one knows for sure.

Joseph "Dutch" Bowers was one of the first prisoners sent to Alcatraz after the island became a federal prison. Dutch had a long criminal record that spanned many, many years. He went to Alcatraz because of a robbery that earned him just $16.38. Dutch believed his twenty-five-year sentence was too long and was determined to get out early.

On April 26, 1936, he decided to leave Alcatraz. When the bell rang at 11:20 that morning, signaling it was time for the inmates to return to the cellblock for lunch, Dutch didn't head for the cellblock. Instead, he started running toward the Model Industries

Building, a prisoner work area. A guard yelled for him to stop.

Dutch ignored the guard and began to climb the chain-link fence. The guard took aim with his gun and fired. Dutch was hit. He toppled over the fence and crashed to the rocks below. Guards recovered Dutch's dead body shortly after.

Over the years, guards and people passing Alcatraz in boats have reported seeing a ghostly figure wandering the island's rugged shore. They say this ghost stands in the same spot where Dutch fell to his death many years ago. Perhaps, like Dutch himself, his spirit was never able to escape the rocky island of Alcatraz.

It's a mystery what happened to the next two escapees, Theodore Cole and Ralph Roe.

At the age of fourteen, Cole killed an Arkansas police officer. Six years later, he was in prison when he stabbed his cellmate to death. Because Cole tried to escape from prison numerous times, he was sent to Alcatraz.

There, Cole worked a job with another inmate named Ralph Roe. Roe was at Alcatraz because he also tried to escape from another prison. It was no surprise, then, when these two like-minded prisoners met up and hatched a plan to try and escape from The Rock.

The men worked in the Model Industries Building. There they discovered that the iron bars covering the windows could be filed and removed. Very slowly, the two prisoners cut through the bars. They careful not to draw attention to what they were doing, using shoe polish and grease to cover the cut marks.

As soon as they had the bars loose enough, they waited for the right time to slip away.

On December 16, 1937, there was a storm in the bay. Thick fog covered the island. A guard saw them working in the tire shop at 1:00 in the afternoon. But by 1:30, the two men were gone.

A massive manhunt began. There was no trace of the pair anywhere on the island. The seas were rough that day because of the storm. In the end, the guards determined there was no way the two men could have survived the mile and half swim to San Francisco. Cole and Roe were listed as missing and presumed dead. The search for them ended.

Today, though most people agree Cole and Roe were swept out to sea, some believe they survived the escape. Maybe, since they worked in the tire building, they used tires to keep themselves afloat in the rough and windy seas and got away. To get off the island, they'd have had to climb down a twenty-foot drop and make it through the bay's famously strong tides. It doesn't seem likely, but because they were never found, no one knows for sure what happened to them.

Perhaps the prisoners—or their ghosts—are

still floating somewhere in San Francisco Bay . . . forever trying to make it back to shore.

Floyd Hamilton, Fred Hunter, James Boarman, and Harold Brest were four inmates who decided that leaving *together* gave them a better chance than escaping alone. In April

1943, they managed to pry open a window in the Model Industries Building where they worked. Using homemade knives, the inmates captured and tied up Officer Smith and Captain Weinhold. Then they stripped to their underwear, escaped through the open window, and made their way down to the shoreline.

These men were prepared. Not only had they covered their bodies in thick grease to help them stay warm in the chilly water, they'd left four cans filled with army uniforms at the beach to use for flotation. The problem was, once they reached the beach, they realized two of the cans were missing. That meant, when they reached the San Francisco shore, only two of them would have clothes.

Before they could come up with another plan, guards began to shoot—Officer Smith had managed to reach his whistle and sound the alarm. The four men jumped into the water and tried to swim away, but none of them got far. Brest was captured and sent back to his cell. Fred Hunter tried to hide in a cave but was recaptured. Floyd Hamilton managed to stay hidden in the same cave and was presumed dead. But three days later, he emerged hungry, cold, and tired. He decided to give up the escape attempt and snuck back into the prison through the same open window, where guards quickly apprehended him.

The fourth man, James Boarman, was shot and disappeared into the depths. His body was never found. Perhaps he escaped after all? Or maybe he drowned. If he did die that day, did his spirit ever find freedom? Or, did it join the other ghosts of Alcatraz, cursed to haunt the island forever? We may never know.

Aaron Burgett and Clyde Johnson tried their luck on September 29, 1958. The two men were assigned clean-up and garbage detail, which meant a guard escorted them outside the security fence while they worked. But the skyline of San Francisco was too tempting.

On a sunny day while picking up trash, Johnson pulled out a knife and threatened the prison guard. The two inmates blindfolded the guard, then tied him to a tree.

Before the escape, Burgett and Johnson managed to make simple "swim fins" out of wood, which they attached to their shoes. They'd also snuck plastic bags out of the prison and inflated them to help them float in the water.

The bay was cold and rough, and though they'd planned their escape well, Johnson gave up immediately. Burgett decided to try to go it alone. He thrashed in the cold water but made slow progress toward the city.

When the guard who had been with the two prisoners didn't report for duty later, some other guards went looking for him. They discovered him tied to a tree and sounded the alarm. Johnson was immediately captured, but there was no sign of Aaron Burgett. One week went by. Then two. Had he made it to freedom?

After fourteen days, Aaron Burgett's body was found pounding against the rocks of the island. He hadn't gotten far. The waves had pushed him back to the prison.

If you are visiting Alcatraz Island, keep your eyes open for the ghost of Aaron Burgett. He is still wearing his prison shirt with the number 991. Be sure to look down at the ghost's feet. When the guards found Aaron Burgett, pieces of the wooden fins were still attached to his shoes.

Some inmates tried to walk away from their

jobs, some tried to cut through bars, and some made swim fins. But others used more violent and vicious ways to try and escape The Rock.

In May 1938, Thomas Limerick, Jimmy Lucas, and Rufus Franklin decided to break out of the prison. Tom Limerick had been sentenced to life at Alcatraz for robbing trains, a bank, and a National Guard armory. Jimmy "Tex" Lucas was only twenty-two years old when he was sent to Alcatraz. He was there for robbery and murder. Rufus "Whitey" Franklin was a convicted bank robber and car thief. Franklin is also known for spending the longest time in a closed solitary confinement cell at Alcatraz. He was a violent man.

Limerick and Lucas planned the escape while working at the Model Industries Building. After they realized they could gain access to the roof of the woodworking shop, the men decided that May 23 would be their last day on the island.

One of the men grabbed a hammer and beat an unarmed officer to death, and then they hurried to the roof. On the way, they tried to get Officer Harold Stites's rifle. Stites took aim and fired. Franklin was wounded. Limerick was killed. And Lucas surrendered.

Ever since this escape attempt, many prison guards working shifts on the tower have reported seeing a prisoner trying to cross the roof. But like clockwork, as the prisoner gets close to the tower, he vanishes. Even today, boaters, tourists, and rangers report seeing an inmate on the prison roof before he disappears into thin air.

Some ghosts get stuck in a loop, repeating their final moments alive over and over for all eternity. Could the prisoner on the roof actually be Tom Limerick, caught in an endless attempt to escape Alcatraz?

Arthur "Doc" Barker, Dale Stamphill, William "Ty" Martin, Rufus McCain, and Henri Young tried to escape Alcatraz on January 13, 1939.

Dale Stamphill was the mastermind of this escape attempt. He got the saws the inmates used to cut through the bars of their cells. He also concocted the wax mixture that covered the cut marks, so no guards knew what was going on.

William "Ty" Martin had been sent to Alcatraz for robbing post offices. He invited Doc Barker to become part of the gang and included him in the prison-break plans. Rufus McCain was a bank robber given a long sentence (ninety-nine years, to be exact) to ensure he died in prison. Henri Young was also a bank robber, known for taking hostages during his robberies. Young was wild and, since he didn't care if they lived or died, had nothing to lose.

It took a while, but the five men managed to use Stamphill's saws to cut the metal bars on the doors to their cells in D block. They covered the cuts with Stamphill's mixture of tar and paint. Then they waited for a thick fog to roll into San Francisco Bay.

On the night of January 12, just after 3:00 in the morning, the convicts pried loose their bars and slipped into the main cellblock corridor. They snuck out of the building and dropped eight feet to the dirt below the prison block.

Barker and Stamphill went one way, down to an alcove where they'd collected driftwood to make a raft. Martin, McCain, and Young went to the docks to find the lumber they'd left there to make their own raft.

The prisoners hadn't left as quietly as they'd planned. While going through the window, there was a popping sound. At first, Junior Officer Hurst ignored it, but then he walked around to check things out. He noticed the bars were missing from Dale Stamphill's cell and sounded the alarm.

Outside, McCain, Young, and Martin managed to launch their raft into the bay. As they got farther out into deeper water, McCain started to panic. He admitted he didn't know how to swim. He forced the others to go back to Alcatraz.

Doc Barker and Dale Stamphill were working 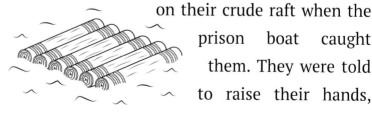 on their crude raft when the prison boat caught them. They were told to raise their hands, but they didn't do it fast enough. Guards shot them both in the legs. Stamphill surrendered. Barker, in pain from his wounds, tried to stand up but couldn't. He was shot below the right eye and later died.

The four recaptured prisoners were sent to solitary confinement and also had their prison time extended. When they came out of solitary, the men went back to work at the Model Industries Building.

In December 1941, Henri Young made a knife blade in the shop and used it to stab Rufus McCain in the stomach. McCain was taken to the prison hospital. He suffered terrible pain for over five hours and eventually died from the stab wound. Some say that Young blamed McCain for the botched escape attempt. Young was so angry at McCain that he killed him in revenge.

A person's spirit sometimes remains behind

in hopes of removing the pain it felt while dying. McCain spent much of his time at Alcatraz in cell 14D, so it makes sense that this cell is said to be one of the most haunted on the island. His spirit is still suffering.

The most violent escape attempt and bloodiest battle in Alcatraz history occurred over two days in May 1946. Known as the "Battle of Alcatraz," the violence that took place at the prison over those forty-eight hours alarmed Alcatraz authorities so much, they called in the U.S. Marines. They'd thought all the prisoners were prepared to fight, when in fact, it was just six men.

It all began when the six tried to escape.

Joe Cretzer was a mean man. He'd been public enemy number four on the FBI list. Sam Shockley was serving a life sentence for his crimes and was known for his violent outbursts in prison. They teamed up with

Miran Thompson, who was in for kidnapping and murder. Marvin Hubbard, Clarence Carnes, and Bernard Coy were also involved. Carnes was the youngest inmate at Alcatraz. He was only eighteen.

Bernard Coy was the mastermind of the escape attempt. Coy had one of the best jobs at the prison. He was in the maintenance department, which meant he had access to the entire cell house. Over several months at work, he noticed that the cells were all empty after lunch. He also tracked the guard on duty and noted his routine.

The men made a plan. While Coy was sweeping the floor, Marvin Hubbard approached a guard named William Miller to tell him that he'd "finished his assignment." While the guard was talking to Hubbard, Coy attacked. Coy then took Guard Miller's uniform.

Coy smeared his own naked body with grease. Using a crude bar spreader that he'd made, he slipped his greasy body though a gap and outside the cellblock. Then he got dressed.

A guard opened the door right on schedule. Coy sprang up and choked the man with his own necktie until he passed out. Then, Coy opened the weapons locker and gave Hubbard and Cretzer riot clubs and handguns.

The convicts rounded up all the guards they could find and locked them in cells 403 and 404. They knew Guard Miller had the keys to the cell house door that led outside. Miller handed them over and the convicts immediately released their friends Thompson, Shockley, and Carnes from their cells. They opened other cells too, trying to get more prisoners to join them. When no one else came along, the six original men continued with their plan.

They struggled to find the right key on Guard Miller's ring to open the cellblock door. They had no way of knowing that the guard had secretly removed the key and hid it in a toilet.

Now prison officials were noticing that some guards hadn't checked in. Other guards were sent to the cellblock to investigate. These guards were forced into the holding cells with the others.

As tensions grew, it was becoming apparent the escape wasn't going to work out the way the prisoners planned. Coy shot at some newly approaching guards through a window.

Cretzer began to worry that the guards they'd captured would identify them. He told the five other escapees to kill all the unarmed guards that they'd trapped in the cells. Carnes didn't want to do it and went back to his own cell in protest. Cretzer was furious. He fired bullets into the cells that held the guards. He didn't even look to see if he'd killed anyone. He just shot the gun, then moved on to meet Coy so they could figure out what to do next.

Hours passed and some prison guards attempted to take back control of the prison, which led to a violent and bloody shoot-out. Three guards were hit and the team had to retreat. The guards sealed the D-block door, trapping the convicts in the cellblock.

Thompson and Shockley, realizing there was no hope for escape, returned to their own cells as if nothing had happened.

That left Coy, Hubbard, and Cretzer loose in the prison.

Finally, prison officials called in the U.S Coast Guard and the Marines to help. The Marines tossed explosive devices into the cellblock and the prison filled with thick smoke, choking everyone, even the inmates not involved. Many inmates tried to shield themselves from the shrapnel and bullets by hiding under their mattresses.

Did the Marines make things worse with their attack? Maybe, but they didn't know what was going on inside. They climbed to the roof of the prison and drilled holes. Grenades were lowered to the cellblock floor. It's estimated that nearly five hundred grenades were used. The Marines thought this would cause the last few men to surrender, but they didn't.

Instead, Cretzer, Coy, and Hubbard escaped into a utility corridor and hid.

After a few quiet hours, the Marines and prison guards entered the cellblock. The building was riddled with bullet holes. Prisoners were hiding under their beds, covering themselves with anything they could find for protection.

Cretzer, Coy, and Hubbard were found dead in the utility corridor. Coy was wearing the stolen guard's uniform and still had a rifle. Cretzer had a pistol and the cellblock keys. Hubbard was the farthest away from the others. It's believed he was the last to die.

The Marines hurried to free the captured prison guards. Guard William Miller died from his injuries. Guard Earnest Lageson was shot in the face. He reported the names of the six men, circling the names of the leaders: Hubbard, Coy, and Cretzer.

Following the Battle of Alcatraz, prison officials sentenced Thompson and Shockley to death. Carnes was spared since he refused to shoot the guards, but he got an extra ninety-nine years added to his sentence. Eighteen guards and almost every inmate who hadn't taken part had some kind of injury.

Today, visitors to Alcatraz can see the signs of the battle. There's still grenade damage on the walls and floors. Bullet holes are also visible. But the more telling signs are the ghosts of Cretzer, Coy, and Hubbard, who many believe have remained on the island ever since that bloody day in May, wandering that same utility corridor and plotting their escape.

As the most famous prisoners to ever attempt escape from Alcatraz, John Anglin, Clarence Anglin, Frank Morris, and Allen West are the subject of many books, movies, and television shows.

On June 11, 1962, these men escaped. Or did they? To this day, what exactly happened to them remains an unsolved mystery.

What we *do* know, however, is that leaving Alcatraz was Allen West's idea.

He'd been painting the prison roof when he realized the ventilation shafts might be a way out. West proposed the idea to brothers Clarence and John Anglin, who had tried to escape from other prisons. The Anglins wanted to include their friend Frank Morris in the plot. Frank was known to be a quick thinker and is often credited with masterminding the entire escape.

Clarence Carnes, one of the original six escapees in the Battle of Alcatraz, had told Frank Morris what they'd learned from that failed attempt. He described large pipes along the utility corridors that could be used to get into the ventilation shafts. Late at night, Morris also discovered that the back wall of his cell was soft enough to dig into.

The four convicts decided if they could each make a hole in their cell's wall big enough to fit through, they'd be able to get around the ventilation ducts and reach the utility corridor behind the cells. They agreed on the plan and every day during "music hour," when the halls filled with the loud sounds of instruments, the four would dig into their walls. Little by little, using spoons they'd stolen from the dining hall as improvised drills, they began to make progress.

When they weren't digging, the men gathered things they could use for rafts and life preservers. They collected fifty raincoats, some stolen and some given by other inmates who knew what they were up to. The Anglins had grown up fishing and exploring swamps in Florida, so they knew how to make a sturdy raft. They also understood ocean currents, which they knew would be useful as they sailed across the bay to San Francisco.

At night, they hid the raft parts in the wall holes.

Frank Morris was able to solve another problem. They didn't want the guards to discover them missing too soon, so they created dummy heads to put in their beds. This way, when the guards peeked into their cells, it looked like they were sleeping. The heads were made of soap, toilet paper, and cement. The Anglins sometimes worked in the barber shop and collected hair for the finishing touch.

The prisoners had a way out, raft parts, and dummies for their beds. Now they needed a way to inflate the rafts. They couldn't spend time blowing them up by mouth. Again, it was Morris who came up with the answer. He had a small accordion that he played during music hour. By removing the keys, he could force air through the accordion and into the raft, like a makeshift air pump.

It was a complicated plan and took eight months to get ready.

One night, the prisoners slipped out of their cells through the holes they'd dug. When

West didn't appear, Frank Morris went to see what happened. West had made his escape hole too small and couldn't fit. The others left him behind.

The Anglins and Morris climbed up the heating pipes to the ceiling, removed the ventilation ducts, then slipped out onto the roof. After a quick dash across, they shimmied down a pipe to the ground. They carried the equipment they'd made with them as they ran to the bay.

The plan was to fill the rafts and sail to Angel Island. There, they'd rest a bit, then swim the rest of the way to San Francisco. They'd steal a car, break into a clothing store, and finally, go their separate ways.

The dummy heads worked as planned. No one noticed the men were missing until morning. Once the alarm sounded, a manhunt began. The first day, the guards found nothing.

Then they found a hand-carved oar floating in the bay. After that, a piece of the raft appeared. Later, the guards found a small watertight bag with an address book, some photographs, and a money order. These items belonged to the Anglins.

A Norwegian freighter reported seeing a body floating near the Golden Gate Bridge. It was thought to be Frank Morris, but the body was never recovered. The FBI used this report as evidence that the three men had drowned, but there was never any proof. After months of investigations, the men were declared "missing, presumed dead."

In a strange twist, the day after the disappearance, a man called a San Francisco law office and said he was John Anglin. He wanted to talk to the U.S. Marshals. The clerk refused to pass along the call. The man asked the operator if she'd seen the news, then hung up.

Alcatraz inmate Clarence Carnes said that he received a postcard a few weeks later. There was no name, just a message: Gone Fishing.

In 2013, the San Francisco police department received a letter from someone claiming to be John Anglin. The letter said the prisoners had made it to freedom, and that now he had cancer. It's unclear if the letter was real or fake.

There have been reported photos of men who say they are John and Clarence Anglin. No one could say for sure if the men escaped or not. And yet, it's been recently reported that the FBI's reports from that night might not be true. Documents have been released showing that the raft was recovered and that three men matching the description of the escapees stole a car just north of San Francisco on the day of the escape.

This is an Alcatraz mystery that may never be solved. The prisoners spent so much time coming up with their plan. They had so many details figured out. In the end, was it worth it? Did they live out the rest of their lives somewhere unknown? Or, were their ghosts doomed to live out their sentences on Alcatraz?

Prison kitchen at Alcatraz

Haunted Places

After twenty-nine years of operation, Alcatraz prison closed in 1963. It was simply too expensive to keep open. The Rock cost nearly three times more to operate than any other federal prison. Ten years later, the National Park Service reopened Alcatraz as a tourist destination. Even though the whole island is only twenty-two acres in area, it now attracts about 1.5 million visitors a year. From the day the public began to visit, staff and tourists have claimed to hear phantom whistles and terrified screams, and to have spotted spirits wandering the old prison hallways and around the island.

The "Dungeon" is one of the scariest spots in all of Alcatraz. This is the last section of the prison that remains from the days when the army owned and operated the island. Back in 1909, when the old Citadel fortress was taken down, the bottom floor was left as a basement for the new cell house. The old moat became a passageway, and the storage rooms became cells.

Prisoners who went into the Dungeon were held in complete darkness. Water dripped from the pipes. There were rats. Convicts had to sleep sitting up, leaning against the walls. Meals were only bread and water. This was all intended so no one would ever want to go there, and just in case a prisoner did end up in the Dungeon, the experience was designed to be so terrible, they'd never want to go back. It wasn't until 1942 that this area was abandoned and new solitary confinement cells were built.

Through the years, tourists have reported hearing shouts and screams coming from the Dungeon, but every time park rangers searched the area after one of these reports, no one was ever found. Officially, the Park Service says there are no ghosts on the island, yet many of the rangers disagree. One ranger said that they went to investigate loud voices and were led on a spine-chilling game of "hide and seek" as the voices calling to her moved around the space. When she reported what happened, others came forward and said they'd had similar experiences.

The Warden's Mansion, built in the 1920s, has its own ghosts. The Hoe House was the mansion where the warden (the person in charge of the prison) and his family lived. There's a story that when Warden Johnston— the first warden at Alcatraz—lived there, a ghost visited his annual Christmas Party. The ghost, a man in a gray suit and hat, stared at the guests for a long time. Ice cold swept the room. Many people witnessed the ghost, but no one knew who it might have been. Before the Warden's Mansion was destroyed in 1970, the ghost had been seen several times. Some say the ghost doesn't care that the mansion isn't there, he's still wandering around the area anyway.

The Alcatraz Lighthouse is strange because it's not a person that haunts it, but rather it's the building itself that is ghostly. The old lighthouse was torn down in the early 1900s. A new lighthouse was built south of the original site. Almost from that very first day, people began reporting that they could still see the old lighthouse. No one knows why a lighthouse would haunt Alcatraz, but there are so many stories about it that it's easy to believe.

One guard in the 1940s said he was walking early in the morning. There was a thick fog that day and it was hard to see. He heard moaning coming from the area between the prison and the new lighthouse. The guard headed over to check it out. Suddenly, something began to shimmer in the mist. The man stumbled backward just as the *old* lighthouse materialized in front of him, including the beacon that used to shine into the bay and a blaring foghorn. The guard quit the next day.

The Laundry Room is said to be another of the most haunted spots on Alcatraz Island. Guards, guests, and guides have all reported smelling smoke, as if there's a fire in the area. The scent is overwhelming.

Sometimes it's so strong, Alcatraz officials evacuate the room and call in the fire department. Oddly, when crews go to inspect, there is never any sign of fire or smoke. In fact, the smell of smoke disappears completely, as if it were never there at all. After many years and countless calls to the fire department, the Laundry Room has become it's own ghostly legend on the island.

The Model Industries Building has seen a lot of death. Because of the violence that took place there, many people consider it a magnet for spirit sightings. Remember that in 1938, Officer Cline was killed there when Limerick, Lucas, and Franklin tried to escape. Henri Young stabbed Rufus McCain in 1941 there as well.

Over the years, reports have been made of a guard haunting the halls. This spirit is usually seen carrying a billy club and patrolling for anything suspicious. The guard glances at tourists, studying them as if they are prisoners. If he's approached, he disappears. The rangers and the employees at Alcatraz today think that maybe this ghost is Officer Royal Cline, searching for the prisoners who killed him.

The ghost of Rufus McCain is also known to lurk in the Model Industries Building. When Henri Young stabbed him, he didn't die right away. McCain was taken to the hospital ward. There, he suffered extreme pain from his gut wound until he finally passed away.

Reports from guests and visitors say they sometimes see a man in a prisoner's uniform running through the building. Before he can reach a door, he stops. The ghost clutches his stomach, then fades away as he falls to the floor. If this is indeed McCain, then his ghost isn't only in the Model Industries Building. After all, it's believed that the red-eyed monster that lurks in cellblock D might *also* be the spirit of McCain . . .

Cellblock D was where the most violent prisoners were held on Alcatraz. The National Park Service welded open some doors to let visitors step inside the cells and get a feel for what it might have been like to be a prisoner there. Cell 14D was the worst of all the cells. There was no sink. No mattress. And no bed. Prisoners were moved there after injuring another prisoner or attacking a guard.

Shortly after these cells were created in 1940, the spirits appeared. Cell 14D had the reputation for being home to a killer ghost. The story goes that there was a prisoner in the 1940s who began to scream that someone was in his cell trying to kill him. He said the demon had red glowing eyes. The guards knew he was alone and ignored his pleas. The next day, when they opened the cell, the man was dead. He had red marks around his throat as if he'd been strangled. But there's more to the story. When the guards did a prisoner count the following day, the strangled man was in the line. But as soon as the guards approached him, he quickly faded away.

The theory is that this ghost is Rufus McCain. He spent so much time incarcerated in this cell that his spirit has remained.

There is no proof that anyone ever died in 14D. The rumors of the killer ghost and the man in line are just stories. And yet, even Bob Davis, the experienced paranormal investigator, had his first strange experience in the cell as a boy. Others have reported spooky sightings in the cell as well. It's said there are odd voices. And echoing screams. We may never know who is haunting cell 14D, but there's no doubt this is one of the most haunted places on the island.

CHAPTER 6

Ghosts of Famous Inmates

ROBERT "THE BIRDMAN" STROUD

Robert Stroud was born in 1890. He committed his first crime when he was nineteen years old. He shot a man and was sentenced to twelve years in prison. During that time, he was always getting into trouble. After one vicious attack, he received more time in prison. But more time in prison only made him a more violent prisoner. He went into a rage in the mess hall and stabbed a guard to death. More than a thousand inmates witnessed Stroud commit that murder. He was convicted of first-degree murder and sentenced to death by hanging. But Woodrow Wilson, the president of the United States at the time, changed the punishment. Instead of hanging, Stroud would spend his life in prison without parole, or early release. He was sent to live in solitary confinement at Leavenworth Prison.

But even prisoners who are sent to live their lives completely alone need fresh air and exercise. One afternoon, Stoud was in the yard when he found an injured canary. Stroud took the canary to his cell and nursed it back to health. That was when he became fascinated with birds.

Stroud began to research ornithology, the scientific study of birds. Over the next thirty years, he wrote two books about birds and was even given equipment for his studies. He was allowed to breed and keep birds in his cell. The books he wrote brought him great respect outside of the prison. He was considered one of the great ornithologists of his time. Eventually, though, it was discovered he was using his equipment not just for research, but also to make alcohol. This was the last straw. In 1942, he was sent to Alcatraz. His days of studying and keeping birds was over.

Stroud was assigned to D block and placed in a special cell for solitary confinement. Without the distraction of his birds, he studied law and wrote two more books. One was an autobiography and the other, a history of the prison system.

Stroud was not a healthy man, and the cold weather at Alcatraz made him very sick. In 1963, Robert Stroud died at a prison hospital in Missouri, but people still see his ghost at Alcatraz. No one can say why his ghost came back to The Rock. Stroud was miserable at Alcatraz. Some claim he appears standing in front of his cell. He stares at the tourists as if studying them. It's said that this ghost even wears his Alcatraz uniform, with number 594, making him easy to identify.

Other times, visitors see ghost 594 in the medical wards where Stroud spent years because of his illnesses. Tourists claim they hear him shuffling cards or speaking in whispers. He was known to play cards and chess with the guards. Some also say that they've seen him pacing the cell room in the early morning. The spirit fades if anyone gets too close.

There was a movie made about Stroud that showed him as a mild-mannered and humane person, but in reality, Stroud was a violent man with a long list of crimes. So, if you see his ghost at Alcatraz, best to steer clear of the "Birdman." This is one ghost to avoid!

CRETZER, COY, AND HUBBARD

The ghosts from The Battle of Alcatraz are often seen at the prison. Cretzer, Coy, and Hubbard are the men who died in a utility corridor after their escape from Alcatraz failed. Some say the three still haunt the corridor.

One of the most famous stories came from an employee who was stationed on the island in 1976. The watchman was near C block when he heard strange noises in the utility corridor. He thought it might be a prowler sneaking around, so he went to check it out. The man stood outside the building and realized the sounds were coming from inside. Very cautiously, he opened the secure door and swung the beam of his flashlight around the room. In an instant, the sounds stopped. But as he walked away, they started up again. He went back for a second look but again found nothing strange. He shook his head as he walked away, wondering if he'd imagined the noises or if they were real.

Today, the utility corridor has a plexiglass door so that tourists can look inside. Guests report hearing noises like the watchman. They say that they feel dizzy if they get too close to the glass barrier. Others report feeling a deep sense of sadness when they near the corridor. Some experience panic and a need to leave right away.

Are the ghosts of Coy, Cretzer, and Hubbard still in the corridor? Are visitors feeling the

panic and dread the prisoners felt when grenades were dropped down to kill them?

AL "SCARFACE" CAPONE

The most notorious gangster in history was Alphonse Capone. His story has inspired books, movies, articles, and even songs. Al Capone began his mob affiliation when he was fifteen. One night, while working at a bar, Capone made a rude remark about the sister of a local gangster, Frank Galluccio. Galluccio pulled out a blade and slashed Capone's left cheek, leaving him with a deep scar. After that, Capone was known as "Scarface."

Scarface grew into a brutal murderer who killed without guilt. He took over and became the mob boss. Capone was involved in some big headline murders, but he was careful; there was never any evidence that pointed to him. To the outside, he looked like a successful businessman. He wore nice suits, fine hats, and didn't hide from the public. He was a family man who enjoyed a night out on the town.

The most well-known case was on February 14, 1929. A gangster named "Bugs" Moran tried to kill off one of Capone's friends. This wasn't the first time Capone and Moran had had problems, but this time, Capone had had enough. He lured men from Moran's gang to a garage, telling them they had whiskey for sale, which was illegal at the time.

Capone's men, dressed like cops, were waiting. The "cops" lined the gangsters up against the wall in a row and gunned them

down. This was known as the Valentine's Day Massacre. Even though Al Capone had arranged it, there was no evidence to pin him to the murders. Everyone—police and other gangs—knew he was responsible, but Capone went free.

In 1931, when Al Capone was finally caught, it was not for any of the bloody crimes he'd committed. He was arrested on twenty-two counts of tax evasion and sentenced to eleven years in prison.

He'd lived an extravagant life of wealth and privilege. Now he was in a cellblock at Alcatraz with regular criminals. Capone was miserable, but he participated in prison life and was granted early release. He died in 1947 at his home in Florida.

So why, if he hated Alcatraz so much, would his ghost choose to haunt the prison?

It's said that Capone's spirit likes to travel. He has been seen in a lot of places, like on a yacht he once owned. Or in the Eastern State Penitentiary, where he spent some prison time.

On Alcatraz, guests and workers have seen the mob boss's ghost near his cell on block B. Sometimes people hear music coming from his cell. He played the banjo. Once, a ranger who was walking the cellblocks after Capone died reported hearing phantom banjo music coming from the mobster's old cell. He went to see if anyone was there. The cell was empty and the music stopped, but as soon as the ranger walked away, the music began again.

Another place people have seen his ghost is near the shower area. Capone liked being alone in prison, and sometimes, when the others were outside in the yard, he was allowed to go to the big shower to practice his banjo. The acoustics were excellent in there.

No one knows why Al Capone's ghost would hang

around Alcatraz since he truly hated the place and was afraid of the other prisoners. Still, many tourists and rangers are certain they've encountered him there. If you're at The Rock, be sure to listen for a banjo, and if you catch the mobster's eye, turn quickly away. You don't want to end up "sleeping with the fishes."

CHAPTER 7

Ghost Stories from Paranormal Investigators

The Rock attracts many paranormal investigators. Because of all the reported ghostly sightings and experiences, it's an exciting place to visit. When they come, they often bring tools to help them communicate with the ghosts.

Bob Davis always remembered being a kid in that Alcatraz cell with a ghost. When he grew up, he decided to become an investigator who searches for ghosts as a job. His company does podcasts, movies, and books explaining their paranormal research.

One way that spirits communicate is through voice recordings. Electronic Voice Phenomenon (EVP) are recordings of sounds believed to be spirit voices. In July 2009, Planet Paranormal went to Alcatraz to make recordings.

The team from Planet Paranormal spread out their equipment in the prison infirmary, trying to get any spirits in the room to talk to them. Suddenly, they all smelled cigarette smoke. A voice cursed a bad word that we cannot repeat here. Everyone assumed it was one of the men from their team, but the guy swore it wasn't him. It's not uncommon for spirits to imitate the living. They sometimes speak in familiar voices. The investigators were certain a spirit was there.

They moved into a cellblock. One of the investigators had a type of radio called a Shack Hack. It sweeps the dial, searching for sounds. When they heard the word "demon," one of the women on the team got scared. The other investigators were used to seeking out spirits, so they weren't surprised. They calmed her down and continued.

They heard the word "jail." Then "hole." This last word was heard near one of the cells where an escape hole had been dug into the wall. The Shack Hack continued to spit out words, one at a time. Finally, at the end of a corridor, the machine said "run." The woman who had been nervous from the beginning had enough. She did exactly what the voice had said and ran from the building!

The other investigators stayed, but the spirits had quieted down. They'd had their fun, scared a woman away, and retreated into the shadows.

In 2014, a British couple was visiting Alcatraz on one of the tours. The woman was taking photos. When she tipped back her camera to look at her pictures, there was an image of a woman in her photo. She looked at the room, then back at the photo. No one was in the room.

In the photo, the spirit is wearing old-fashioned clothing. The tourist said that she didn't believe in ghosts until that moment.

Who might that woman be? Do you remember the story of the nurse who died on the island? Was it her?

Planet Paranormal had many experiences with ghosts on the island, but one experience will stay in their memories forever. There are three rooms near the medical isolation wards where sick and contagious prisoners were treated. In one of these rooms, Planet Paranormal set up recording equipment and began an audio session. They tried to call out to spirits, but none answered.

Brian, one of the members of the team, suddenly noticed his batteries were low. He went to sit on a bench just outside the door. The other investigators went with him. After they left, the chairs the investigators had been sitting on were mysteriously rearranged. The investigators thought this was a sign that a ghost wanted to talk, but again, they couldn't get any to speak to them.

They decided to go out by the bench again.

The same thing happened. The chairs in the room began to move, scraping the floor as a ghostly presence rearranged them, one by one.

The investigators returned and Bob decided to talk to the ghost. He told the ghost that if he wanted them to leave, all it had to do was say so. Just one word, and they'd be gone. Apparently, the spirit wasn't the talking kind. Another investigator named Ash was sitting in a chair near the wall. Suddenly, Ash was shoved backward three feet and hit the wall with a crash. At the same time Ash was shoved, a deep voice shouted, "*Get out!*"

The investigators hurried to pack up and leave, just as Bob had promised. The strangest thing was that afterward, Bob sometimes got angry at the team for no reason. It was as if some of the ghost's emotions had rubbed off on the investigator. Luckily, the feeling passed in time, but the ghost had shown its power.

There are so many ghosts on Alcatraz that it's impossible to investigate all the reported sightings. The rangers hear voices. The tourists see spirits. Inside the buildings and outside the old fort, there is paranormal activity in every corner.

Some people are excited to talk to ghosts. Others are afraid of what they might hear or who they might see. Paranormal investigators aren't scared. They would like to spend more nights on the island. They want to make recordings and try to talk to angry spirits. Investigating ghosts on Alcatraz is not like finding friendly, helpful spirits. The souls that remain at The Rock are predominantly convicts, criminals,

and those who were so dangerous they needed more than just your average prison. These convicts needed to be locked away without any chance of escape.

Maybe someday investigators will know more about the restless spirits that roam the island, but until then, they collect stories. Everyone the investigators talk to agrees

Alcatraz is one of the most haunted places in America.

Who knows what you might find there.

The question is . . . are you brave enough to visit?

A Ghostly Goodbye

It's up to you to decide what you think about the strange things that happen on Alcatraz Island. Are the voices, sounds, and ghostly appearances real? Or just imagined?

It's immediately clear to those who tour Alcatraz Island that The Rock is a cold and sad place. The blistering winds and foggy sky are a constant reminder of the island's somber history.

It's easy to imagine the Ohlone hiding from Spanish missionaries, fearful that they'll be discovered and killed.

The fortifications that once protected the bay are surrounded by craggy rocks and hidden caves that have seen their share of desperation and death.

Today, the hallways in the federal prison, where some of the United States' most notorious and violent criminals were held, are quiet and empty. No one lives behind those steel bars anymore. There's no one in the infirmary. No one in the corridors or yard. The walls and cells alone tell the stories of the notorious criminal masterminds who once filled the halls.

A trip to Alcatraz Island will push you to think about what you believe. Reading these stories might keep you awake, hiding under your covers with a flashlight. Perhaps the next time you hear a bump in the night, you'll wonder: *Are ghosts real . . . or not?*

New York Times bestselling author **Stacia Deutsch** has written more than three hundred children's books, including *The Jessie Files*, a spin-off of the beloved *Boxcar Children* mystery series. Stacia lives in Temecula, California, where she is a member of the historical society. She loves hearing spooky stories! Find her at www.staciadeutsch.com. Instagram @staciadeutsch_writes and www.facebook/staciadeutsch.

Check out some of the other *Spooky America* titles available now!

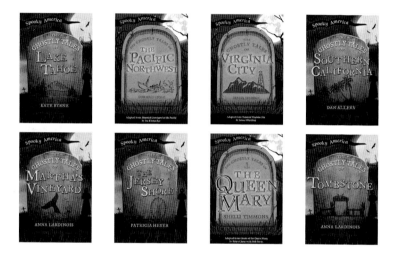

Spooky America was adapted from the creeptastic *Haunted America* series for adults. *Haunted America* explores historical haunts in cities and regions across America. Here's more from the original *Ghosts and Legends of Alcatraz* authors Bob Davis and Brian Clune: